This book belongs to

About Katha

Katha, a nonprofit organisation working with and in story and storytelling since 1988, is one of India's top publishing houses. Katha's main focus is on introducing an array of writings from the many oral and written traditions of India to children, ages 0-17. Classy productions, child-friendly layouts and superb illustrations go in tandem with excellent writing. Katha works with 6,000 Friends of Katha and a growing pool of writers, translators and literary enthusiasts. Our constant striving is for greater reach and impact amongst teachers and students, policy makers and the corporate sector.

Our mission: To enhance the joys of reading. To help every child realise his/her potential through community enriching, quality learning so that no child lives in poverty. To help break down gender, social, cultural and economic stereotypes through story and storytelling. And to enhance the role of translation as a counter-divisive tool in nation building.

Our belief: Stories help create friendships of a rare kind to culturelink people, faiths and creative impulses. Stories are the life-savers of future nations.

Our credo: Uncommon creativities for a common good.

Ka

THE STORY OF GARUDA

based on the english translation by
of the italian original by
Roberto Calasso

Retold by
Geeta Dharmarajan

Illustrated by
Suddhasattwa Basu

Suddenly an immense eagle darkened the sky. Its bright black, almost violet feathers made a moving curtain between clouds and earth. And hanging from its claws were an elephant and a turtle. These two animals skimmed the mountaintops, immense and stiff with terror, for it seemed the bird meant to use the peaks as pointed knives to tear them to pieces. Only occasionally did the eagle's far-seeing eye flash out from behind the thick fronds of the huge branch it held tight in its beak.

Garuda flew and remembered. Flying was the best way of thinking, of thinking things over, wasn't it? He remembered the story that his mother had told him as soon as he was born.

It was only a few days since
he had hatched from his egg, bright as
the sun, each of his feathers shimmering as if lit
by a thousand rays. And already so much had happened.
Who was the first person he'd seen? His mother, Vinata.
Beautiful in her tininess, she was sitting on a stone, watching
his egg hatch. Still, very still. Hers was the first eye Garuda
held in his own. And at once he knew that that eye was his
own. Deep within it was an ember that glowed in the breeze.
So like the one that burned beneath his own feathers.

And there, opposite his mother was another woman, sitting
on another stone. How exactly like Ma she looked, except
that she wore a black bandage over one eye. And she too was
lost in thought.

On the ground before her, the baby Garuda saw a great
tangle, slowly heaving and squirming. His perfect eye looked
deeply at the heap, trying to understand. They were snakes!
Black snakes, knotted and separate, coiling and uncoiling.

Garuda could make out a thousand snake eyes. Coldly
watching him. And then from behind him came a voice.
"They are your cousins, child. And that is my sister, Kadru.
We are their slaves."

These were the first words his mother spoke to him.

Garuda didn't know what was happening. Looking at him, his mother said:

My child, it's time for you to know who you are. You are born to a mother who is a slave. But I too was free once.

Once long ago, I and my sister Kadru were given in marriage to Kasyapa, the great rishi. Kasyapa was slow, strong and silent. But he understood everything. He loved Kadru and me. He gave us the few things we wanted. Otherwise, he sat still for hours and hours, for days and months and years, unmoving. We had no idea what he was doing. My sister and I longed to be doing something too, with ourselves.

One day he called us and he said, "You have been good to me. I will give you one grant each before I go away into the forest. Ask for anything you want."

At once we, Kadru and I, thought of ourselves all alone, in the midst of these empty marshes, the deep forests and thorny bushes and the endless sand dunes. And Kadru said quickly, "I want a thousand children, each shining like the sun."

Kasyapa nodded his head.

I too was quick to decide. I want just two children. But they must be more beautiful than Kadru's, I said. And more powerful.

Kasyapa raised his heavy eyelids. "You will have one and a half," he said.

And he set off into the forest with his stick. We never saw him again.

Ma went on: My child, I have kept watch over your egg for five hundred years. I didn't want the same thing to happen to you as happened to your brother. Aruna.

I looked curiously at her. A brother?

Yes, said my mother. But you see, I was impatient. I opened his egg too soon. And then I suddenly understood what, many years after that sad day, a rishi would say to me. He, pale and thin, coming from a distant land, said, "Being impatient is the only sin."

There was Aruna, my first son, the lower half of his body still unformed. He looked straight at me and he said, "You'll be your sister's slave for five hundred years. Till your second son, my brother, saves you." And then he flew away. Now you can see him cross the sky every day. He is Surya's charioteer. He has never spoken to me again.

Ma went on: So there we were, Kadru and me. The only human beings, with a thousand black snakes about us, all of them the same. And you growing inside your egg, that lay unseen in a pot of steaming clay.

Even as you grew, trouble was brewing in the kingdom of Indra. One awful day, Indra earned the wrath of a rishi. And from that day on, life for the gods began to dull. There was no happiness or any magic in their lives.

They had to do something! When they asked Vishnu, he said, "O devas! Churn the Sea of Life. It will yield soma, the water of life. This will make you strong again and deathless. We need the asuras with us. We can do it only with their help."

Now, the gods looked with hatred on the asuras. And what use was a fight if what you want isn't there to fight for? Both of them didn't have the soma. So the devas asked the asuras

for their help. And, gloomily, they met on Mount Meru, where the peak passes through the vault of the heavens to become the only part of this world that belongs to the other.

Vinata fell silent.

Garuda respected her silence for a long time. Then, impatient, he said, "Ma, Ma, you still haven't told me how you became a slave to your sister!"

Vinata said:

The asuras and the devas got busy churning the ocean. For years and years they worked …

One evening we, Kadru and I, were walking together, kicking the waves of the ocean, our eyes searching the waters, for the creatures of the deep, for pearls. Suddenly, we saw a strange glow in the depths of the waters. But standing there, staring at the waters, Kadru and I didn't know where the light came from. Far far away was the ocean's end. Where sea joined sky I saw two different lights. One sharp bright line separated them.

Then out of the ocean sprang a beautiful white horse! It raised its hooves over waters and sky and leapt into the empty sky. Child, this was how I discovered amazement!

And then, suddenly, we saw something dark next to the bright horse.

A log?

Its tail?

Garuda stopped her. "Who was the horse?" he asked.

I didn't know then, but it was Uccaihsravas. He was born when the ocean was churned for the amrita.

As he sat listening to his mother, Garuda was like a little boy who hears something for the first time, something that will remain large and dark, with him for his whole life.

"Ma," he said, "I shall not ask you anything more about the horse, but tell me your story."

Vinata had become very, very quiet. But she soon began talking again, slowly, trying to be clear and to say only the little that could be said at this point. She spoke with her eyes on the ground, almost unaware of the royal presence of her son, or his feathers quivering.

We were looking at the white horse. The more it enchanted me, the greater anger I felt for my sister. I said: Ai One-Eye, can you see what colour that horse is?

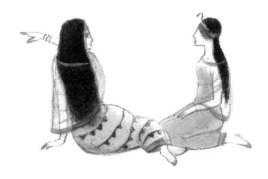

Kadru didn't answer. The black bandage leaned forward.

Then I said, Want to bet? The one who gets the horse's colour right will be mistress of the other.

The following morning, at dawn, we were together again, watching the sky. And once again the horse appeared against the background of sea and sky.

I shouted, It's white. Silence. Kadru, I repeated, don't you think it's white?

To this day I have never seen such a nasty look in her eye.

Kadru said, "It's got a black tail."

We'll go and see, I said, and whichever of us is wrong will be the other's slave.

"So be it," Kadru said.

We took flight, side by side. The creatures of the deep flashed above the waters, surprised to see two women in flight. We paid no attention. The only thing in the world that mattered to us was our game. When we reached the horse, I stroked its

white rump.

As you see, I said to Kadru.

"Wait," said One-Eye. And she showed me a few black hairs her deft fingers picked out from among all the white of the creature's tail.

Some say that those hairs were nagas, faithful to their mother Or that there was only one black hair, the Terrible Snake, Karkotaka. Others say that Uccaihsravas has black hairs mixed in with the white. Who knows? But, "I've beaten you. The sea is my witness. Now you are my slave," said Kadru. "Till you get me the amrita from Indra's guarded kingdom!"

It was then that I, with a suddenly heavy heart, realized what debt is. For five hundred years I have felt its weight.

You, Garuda, are my son. And you were born to set me free. All children are born to set their parents free. And there is only one way you can do that. Bring the amrita and give it to the nagas. You'll find the soma in the sky, child, guarded over by Indra and all the gods, and all the other powerful beings. It's the amrita you must win.

They sat, face-to-face. Garuda, a baby still, but a full mountain of feathers. Vinata, a minute, sinuous creature.

"I'll go to Devaloka and win this amrita, Ma," said Garuda, pained by what had happened to his mother. "But first I must eat."

And Vinata said: Go to the middle of the ocean, my son. There you'll find the land of the Nisadas. You can eat as many of them as you want. They don't know the Vedas. But remember, Never kill someone who's a brahman. He is fire, a blade, poison. Never, never ever do that, even if seized by anger. It will only hurt you!

Garuda listened, even more serious.

"But what is a brahman, Ma?" he asked. "How do I recognize one?"

So far Garuda had seen nothing but black, coiled nagas and those two women who hated each other. He did not know what his father looked like. A brahman? What on earth can that be? wondered Garuda.

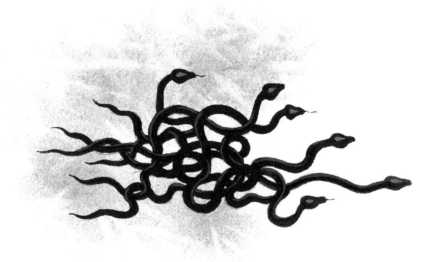

If you feel a brand of fire in your throat, said Vinata, that's a brahman. Or if you suddenly feel you've swallowed a sharp hook, that's a brahman.

Garuda stared straight at her. So you can't tell a brahman until you've almost swallowed him, he told himself.

But already his wings were stretching out. Garuda was eager to find food. And all the fourteen worlds shook when he spread his wings and took off for the land of the Nisadas.

The Nisadas didn't even see Garuda coming. Blinded by the wind and dust that Garuda's wings churned up, they were sucked by the thousands into a dark cavity that opened behind his beak. They plunged deep into the belly of the giant bird, as if into a well. But one of them managed to hang on to that endless wall. With his other hand he held a young woman with snaky hair tight by the waist.

Garuda, who was gazing ahead with his beak half open, suddenly felt something burning in his throat.

That's a brahman, he thought. And, "O Brahman!" he shouted in a quivering voice. "I don't know you, but I don't mean you any harm. Do come out of my throat."

And from Garuda's throat came a shrill, steady voice. "I won't! Unless I can bring my Nisada woman with me. She's my bride."

"Whatever you please," said Garuda.

Soon he saw them climbing onto his beak, taking care, fearful of getting hurt. Garuda watched curiously as he saw them sliding down his feathers. Now, he thought, finally I'll know what a brahman looks like.

The brahman was thin, bony, dusty, his hair woven and matted, his eyes sunken and vibrant. His long, determined fingers never let go of the wrist of the Nisada woman. She was beautiful. She reminded Garuda of his Ma and his mean aunt, Kadru.

He looked at her, worried, as those two tiny beings hurried off, quick and impatient. Had he already swallowed up thousands of women like her?
He hoped not.

Suddenly, he felt he must talk to his father, whom he'd still not seen. He stretched his wings. And another whirlwind devastated the earth as Garuda flew off to find his father, Kasyapa.

When Garuda came crashing down, Kasyapa was watching a line of ants. He paid no attention to his son, nor to the sound that announced his arrival. But Garuda wasn't eager to speak either. He sat watching his father whom he was seeing for the first time, his wrinkled, polished skull, his noble arms. He thought, "He is my father, but he is the father of all living things on earth"

And looking carefully at Kasyapa, Garuda thought, "Now I know who a brahman is. It is one who sticks in your throat as my mother said. But it is also one who is like my father. One who doesn't lie. Is patient. Mild and caring."

Garuda wanted to be like that.

After a day's silence, Kasyapa looked up at Garuda.

"How is your mother?" he asked. But immediately, as if he already knew the answer to his question, he said, "Garuda, go find the elephant and the turtle who are quarrelling in a lake. They will be your food. You can rest on my friend the Rauhina, to eat. But on

this kind-hearted tree live sixty thousand of my friends. Be careful you don't hurt the Vaalakhilyas. They are no bigger than half my thumb. The world lives on because of the pure-hearted Vaalakhilyas who spend all their time in prayer, hanging head downwards ..." said Kasyapa.

And that is how Garuda found his food – the elephant and the turtle. And now, here was he, the two animals, immense and stiff with fear, tight in his claws, thinking, thinking. Where were those Vaalakhilyas? No sooner was one puzzle solved, another bigger thing turned up. Garuda flew on, his mind still mulling over this new problem when his wing skimmed the huge tree Rauhina and he heard a voice:

"By all means rest on a branch and eat. Before you were born you sat here on me, along with a friend who looked exactly like you. Remember? Perched on opposite branches, you never left each other! You couldn't fly about the world then, because I was the world!"

Garuda settled on a branch. Buried in the leaves of the Rauhina, he felt at home but couldn't understand why. His birthplace was only sand, stone, and nagas. But this tree protected him on every side with ribbons of emerald that softened the sharp light of the sky. Hmm ...

Garuda settled down comfortably to feast on the elephant and the turtle, now on their backs on this branch that was a hundred miles long. With great concentration, he was choosing the spot where he would sink his beak, when he heard a sudden crash.

The branch had snapped.

Shame and guilt overcame Garuda. He had done something awful! And it was all the more so because he had not meant it. And the Vaalakhilyas who prayed constantly, hanging head downwards from the branch, where were they?

With one quick swirl, Garuda caught the broken branch in his beak. If he could help it, not one friend of his father's would be hurt.

And so he fluttered into the sky, the elephant and the turtle still in his claws. He was lost. He didn't know where to go. He sensed he was about to make a fatal mistake.

Suddenly from the branch came a hiss. At first he thought it was the wind. He looked at the twigs.

Upside down among the leaves, dangled scores of people, each no taller than a thumb. Their bodies were perfectly formed and almost transparent, like wings of flies.

"Noble Vaalakhilyas," said Garuda, "the last thing I want is to hurt you."

He was answered by a mocking rustle. "That's what you all say ..."

Garuda could make out a voice speaking.

"What lasts and lasts is as tiny and delicate as a syllable. You should know that. The tiny is seen as unimportant. So it is uncared for ..."

"Not by me," said Garuda. But he found that his flight was suddenly more awkward. He floated in the skies, taking the greatest possible care not to shake the branch he held in his beak. Unsure of himself, he studied the mountains, looking for a clearing large and soft enough for him to put down these great rishis who did no evil. But he couldn't find one.

Perhaps he would circle and circle the sky till he finally died?

It was then that a huge mountain lifted its head ahead of him. It was the powerful Gandhamadana on which his father Kasyapa prayed!

Garuda flew around the peak, slowly and cautiously, wondering if he should try one last exploration, when he recognized the polished head of his father. Kasyapa was sitting by a pond on the slopes of the Gandhamadana that were veiled in shadow. Garuda hovered over him, without making a sound.

After a long while of silence, Kasyapa said, "Child, you've done the right thing ..."

Garuda was still hovering above his father, terrified, when he heard Kasyapa's voice change. He was speaking in a soft whisper to the Vaalakhilyas, as if to friends. And a second later, Garuda saw the Vaalakhilyas separate themselves from the branch. Like tiny, dry leaves, grey and dusty, they turned slowly in the air and settled next to Kasyapa. Soon they had disappeared among the blades of grass, heading toward the Himalaya.

Garuda watched them go, worried for their safety.

Long after the last of the Vaalakhilyas had disappeared, he said, "Father, you saved me."

Without looking up, Kasyapa answered, "I saved you because you saved yourself."

"Who are the Vaalakhilyas?" asked Garuda, in a soft voice.

Kasyapa laughed at his little son who towered over him. "Listen to the story," he said.

One day I had to celebrate a sacrifice, do a yagna. I had told Indra and the other gods to find me some wood. Indra was proud of his strength. As he was walking along, he saw a puddle. Something was moving in it - the Vaalakhilyas. They were trying to bring in firewood, too, for the yagna, but it was hard going for them. Moving in single file, they held a blade of grass on their shoulders, like a log, and at the same time were struggling to get out of the mud. Indra stopped to watch, shaking with laughter. He was drunk with power and, just as they were about to get out, he pushed those Vaalakhilyas back into the puddle with his heel. Laughing.

The following day the Vaalakhilyas visited me. They said, "We've come to give you half our tapas. As you know it is the result of many, many years of prayers. It's the purest tapas, something the world has never seen. Now we want to pour some into you so that you can create a being who will be a new Indra, who will bring to an end the arrogant and cowardly Indra. Such a one shall be your son."

But Indra cannot be thrown out by any god or human, I said.

"Then he shall be an Indra of the birds!" they said.

And so you were born, son, glowing, each of your feathers shimmering as if lit by a thousand rays of the sun, burning with the fire of the noble Vaalakhilyas. Garuda had almost forgotten that he was still hovering in the air, still holding the elephant and the turtle. Not to mention that cumbersome branch, still clenched in his beak. Garuda didn't dare do anything further on his own. If he dropped the branch on one of the nearby mountains, even the most barren, and crushed so much as a single living being, hidden in the vegetation, what then?

Kasyapa understood his son's problem.

Fly away, Garuda, Kasyapa said. Go north. When you find a mountain covered with nothing but ice and riddled with caves like dark eye sockets, leave the branch there. That's the only place where there's no risk of killing anyone.

Garuda flew off at once, thinking, How many things are happening! So many stories, one inside the other, every link hiding yet more stories … And I've hardly hatched from my egg!

But he felt good about the future. He would find a place with no living creatures. He would stop and think things over once he reached there.

"No one has taught me anything. Everything has been shown to me. It will take me all my life to begin to understand what I've learnt. To understand, for example, what it means to say that I have the fire of the Vaalakhilyas to do good …"

He was even happier, when a barrier of pale blue ice and snow filled his eyes. It would have blinded any other eye, but Garuda's.

The branch of the tree Rauhina fell with a thud. Then down plunged the elephant and the turtle on to gleaming snow.

At last … Around him on an endless white carpet lay the remains of the elephant and the turtle.

"And now, action!" said Garuda as he rose in flight, off to win the soma to free his mother.

At that very moment one of the gods noticed something odd in the heavens. The garlands had lost their fragrance, a thin layer of dust had settled on the buds. It was a moment of pure terror in Indraloka.

And then … the skies shook. Then came the rains of fire. Then meteors. Then whirlwinds. And then the thunder.

Indra hurled his lightning bolt as Garuda invaded the sky.

The lightning bounced off Garuda's gleaming feathers.

"How can that be?" said Indra to Brihaspati, chief priest of the gods. "This is the lightning bolt that split the heart of every one of my enemies. And Garuda tosses it aside like a straw?"

The gods knew they were going to lose. They hurried to get away. But every flap of Garuda's wings unleashed whirlwinds of dust. Maddening! Dust in the heavens? It was the ultimate disgrace …

Finally, even the guardians of the soma were overcome. In vain they loosed their arrows. An arrow from Krisanu, the footless archer touched one of Garuda's feathers. The feather spun majestic in the sky, as it fell.

But Garuda took no notice. There was still the hardest of tests to overcome. He had to find the soma that would free his mother from her bondage.

And then at last …

On the summit of the heavens he found a metal wheel, its sharp spokes spinning endlessly. Behind the wheel he could just see a glow: a gold cup, or rather two cups, one turned upside down upon the other, their rims jagged and sharp. These cups too

went round and round, endlessly. They opened and closed in a rocking motion. When they closed, their rims fit perfectly together. Between the wheel and the cups hissed two serpents.

Garuda tossed dust in their eyes and concentrated. He must slip between the wheel's blades, get his beak between the rims of the two cups, and snatch the glow he had glimpsed within.

Then escape.

But everything had to happen in no more than the blinking of an eye. On that tiny fraction of time depended the fate of his mother, indeed of the world. And Garuda did it. In a flash, the cup was in his beak.

And now, soma found, Garuda headed back to earth, the nectar clutched in his enormous beak. Not once did he think of drinking the soma that dripped from his beak. Not once did he think

of anything but of his mother. And the nagas.

And so it was that Garuda finally succeeded. His mother was free! Garuda said, "Ma, climb on my back."

And then, Garuda flew, so large and happy, blotting out the sun and darkening the sky. To wander over forests and plains, over the ocean, happy and carefree with his mother. There was a long long way for Garuda to go, he had so much to learn, so many questions remained unanswered. He would, he decided, go sit on the Rauhina tree to learn the Vedas. He would spend many, many days and months and years in prayer and meditation, like his father. But for this moment, he was happy.

Roberto Calasso is writer par excellence from Italy, author of evocative fables such as Ka and The Ruin of Kasch. His book The Marriage of Cadmus and Harmony won France's Prix Veillon and the Prix du Meilleur Livre Etranger.

Geeta Dharmarajan writes for children and adults. Her works have been published in India and abroad. She is Executive Director, Katha.

Tim Parks, best known as writer and translator has written ten novels and three nonfiction accounts. His many translations from the Italian include works by Moravia, Tabucchi, Calvino and Calasso. He lectures on literary translation in Milan.

Suddhasattwa Basu is a renowned illustrator, painter and maker of animation films for television. For Song of the Scarecrow, a picture book written and illustrated by him, he won the ChitraKatha Award and recieved an honourable mention at the Biennial of Illustration 2003, Bratislava.

KATHA

First published © Katha, 2004
Copyright © Katha, 2004
Original text copyright © Roberto Calasso, 2004
Retold text copyright © Geeta Dharmarajan, 2004
Illustrations copyright © Suddhasattwa Basu, 2004
All rights reserved. No part of this book may be reproduced or utilized in any form without the prior written permission of the publisher.
ISBN 978-81-89020-04-0

KATHA is a registered nonprofit devoted to enhancing the joys of reading amongst children and adults. Katha Schools are situated in the slums and streets of Delhi and tribal villages of Arunachal Pradesh.

A3 Sarvodaya Enclave, Sri Aurobindo Marg
New Delhi 110 017

Phone: 4141 6600 . 4182 9998

E-mail: marketing@katha.org, Website: www.katha.org

Ten per cent of sales proceeds from this book will support the quality education of children studying in Katha Schools. Katha regularly plants trees to replace the wood used in the making of its books.